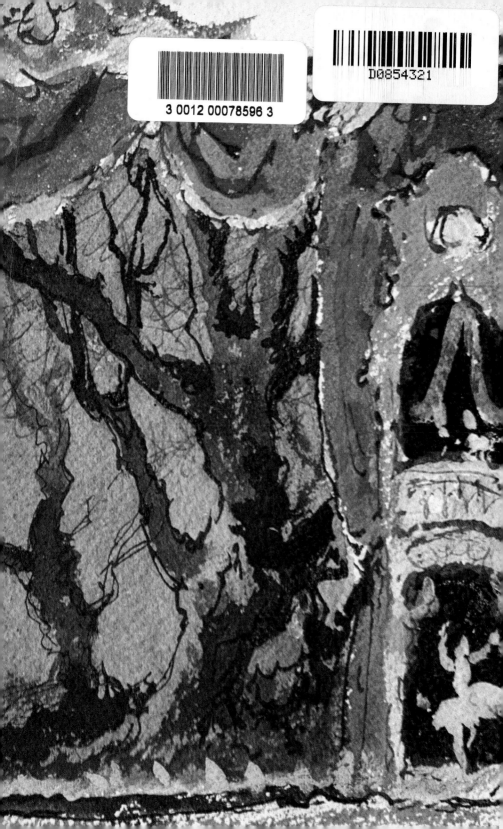

Giselle

STORIES OF THE BALLETS

Giselle

Geoffrey Ashton

Aurum Press

First published in Great Britain 1985
by Aurum Press Ltd, 33 Museum Street,
London WC1A 1LD

Edited and designed and illustrated by
E.T. Archive Ltd, 15 Lots Road, London SW10 0QH

Designed by Julian Holland

Picture research by Anne-Marie Ehrlich

ISBN 0 948149 03 5

Colour separations by La Cromolito, Milan

Phototypeset by Tradespools Ltd, Frome, Somerset

Printed in Belgium by Henri Proost

Endpapers: Design for Act II of *Giselle* by Alexandre Benois
            (Private collection)

Title-page: Marguerite Porter in *Giselle* Act I. Royal Ballet, 1980
             (Reg Wilson)

Contents

The Plot **6**
Romantic Ballet **12**
The Origins of Giselle **20**
The Music **24**
The Choreography **30**
The Original Designs **36**
The Survival of Giselle **42**
Index and Acknowledgments **48**

The Plot

Act I

A pleasantly wooded valley of the Rhine in Germany, one early morning in October. To the left is a thatched cottage covered in vines and clambering flowers. To the right is a smaller cottage, less picturesque than the other. In the distance are vineyards, and a feudal castle.

Hilarion, a gamekeeper in love with Giselle, enters. He looks tenderly at Giselle's home, the cottage on the left, and gestures angrily at the other where Loys, his rival in love, lives. The door of Loys' cottage begins to open and Hilarion hides. He sees Loys emerge, a handsome young

Set design for Act I by Alexandre Benois, signed and dated 3 December 1948. Based on the original design of 1910 for the Ballets Russes production at the Paris Opéra

man dressed as a simple peasant, followed by Wilfrid, who is much more richly dressed, with a cloak, a sword and a feathered cap. Hilarion is surprised to see Loys sharply, even rudely, reject the advice that Wilfrid is evidently offering him and his surprise turns to amazement when he sees Wilfrid make a low, even servile, bow to Loys and swiftly depart at a gesture from the peasant. Hilarion is unaware that the great and powerful Duke Albrecht of Silesia, who lives in the castle on the horizon, has adopted peasant clothes and the name of Loys in order to pay court to Giselle, the prettiest of his subjects. However, Hilarion begins to suspect that Loys is not quite the man he seems.

Loys crosses the stage and knocks on the door of Giselle's cottage. She rushes out happily and the two lovers embrace. Loys assures her of his love but Giselle tests him by picking the petals from a flower, playing a game of he-loves-me, he-loves-me-not. The petals tell her that Loys does not love her. He picks up the discarded flower and, with further plucking, manages to produce a favourable result. Giselle is greatly relieved, and she and Loys dance to celebrate. They end up in each other's arms and Hilarion, jealous of their happiness, emerges from his hiding-place to remonstrate. Giselle shrugs off his anger, telling him that she loves Loys and does not care who knows it, while Loys finds Hilarion's behaviour irritating and pushes him away. Hilarion goes off with threats and dark looks.

A group of village girls arrives at Giselle's cottage. They are carrying baskets to hold the grapes they are about to harvest and urge Giselle to go with them to the vineyards. She thinks it would be a much better idea to dance, and begins to perform on her own to encourage the others. They soon join in, forgetting all about their work. They stop when Berthe, Giselle's mother, emerges from the cottage. She scolds Giselle for wasting time instead of working and tells her that if she is not careful she will end up as a Wili, having to dance for ever after her death. Giselle tosses her warning aside although the villagers tremble at the thought of the Wilis. Loys is extremely concerned when Berthe tells him that Giselle is very delicate and could easily die from too much vigorous exercise.

The sound of a distant hunting-horn interrupts Berthe's warnings and gives Loys another cause for worry. He goes with the villagers to the vineyards while Giselle, blowing a farewell kiss, disappears into the cottage with her mother. Hilarion uses this opportunity to solve the mystery of the imperious Loys and furtively climbs in through the window of his rival's cottage.

A hunting party arrives, led by the Prince of Courland and his daughter Bathilde. They are tired and a huntsman knocks at Giselle's door to ask for refreshment. Giselle offers food and drink while admiring Bathilde's rich velvet riding-habit. Bathilde is amused at Giselle's artlessness and gives her a gold chain. The Prince dismisses his huntsmen and tells them that he will blow the horn left outside the cottage when he wants them. He then goes inside. Bathilde asks Giselle about herself and learns that she adores dancing and is in love with Loys, who lives over the way. Bathilde replies that she too is in love and is about to be married to her fiancé, a young duke. She promises Giselle a dowry and then joins her father in the cottage as Giselle goes off to find Loys and tell him her good news.

Hilarion, who has been listening, appears at the door of Loys' cottage holding a fine sword and a richly embroidered cloak. Now he is sure that Loys is a seducer in disguise.

Loys and Giselle enter from different directions and fall into each other's arms as the villagers return from the vineyards. Giselle is crowned Queen of the Vintage and the celebrations begin with Giselle leading Loys in a dance followed by the rest of the company. The dance ends with a kiss for Giselle from Loys. This is too much for Hilarion and he leaps into the middle of the stage with the sword and cloak, telling Giselle that Loys is a vile seducer, a nobleman in disguise, and that only he, Hilarion, loves her truly. He shows her the sword and the cloak and tells her where he found them. Giselle is deeply shocked but Loys reassures her. Hilarion, seeing that his news is not having the required effect, decides to take sterner measures. Remembering the Prince's orders to his huntsmen, he picks up the horn outside Giselle's cottage and blows it.

The huntsmen come running and the Prince and Bathilde emerge from the cottage. Hilarion indicates Loys at Giselle's feet and the entire hunting party pays its respects to the young Duke. Giselle is horror-struck, realizing that Loys is the young nobleman Bathilde is to marry. Giselle staggers, trying to repeat the steps of the earlier dance with her lover. She puts his hand on her heart but then thrusts him away, picks up his sword and tries to plunge it into her breast. Loys pulls it away but clearly Giselle has lost her reason. She dances in a frenzy round the stage before stopping suddenly, tottering a few steps and dropping into her mother's arms. Loys attempts to revive Giselle but she is dead. In despair he tries to kill himself with his sword. He is stopped by the Prince and the curtain falls.

Giselle is made Queen of the Vintage, Act I. Engraving by Lavielle after J. B. Giraldon for Les Beautés de l'Opéra 1845, inspired by the original Paris production in 1841

Act II

A mysterious forest-clearing beside a lake. Reeds and rushes and wild flowers cover the banks and tall birches spring from the damp undergrowth. Weeping willows droop into the still water which is covered with water-lilies. To the left a cypress stands over a moss-covered mount, a lonely grave surmounted by a marble cross inscribed 'Giselle'. As the mist rises from the lake, the scene is lit by the bluish light of the moon.

Flashes of lightning portend a storm as Hilarion and a group of huntsmen arrive. Hilarion tells the others that this part of the forest is haunted by the Wilis and shows them Giselle's grave. He reminds them that she, like all Wilis, spent her life dancing. Midnight strikes in the distance and the terrified huntsmen flee.

Myrtha, Queen of the Wilis, appears, spreading a mysterious luminescence about the glade. She flits about in the moonlight and, plucking a branch of rosemary, summons the Wilis to join their Queen in their nightly dance. She tells them that a new sister is to be admitted that evening and she indicates Giselle's tomb. She passes her sceptre of rosemary over the grave and Giselle slowly rises out of it, covered in a thin shroud. At a touch from Myrtha the shroud falls off and Giselle sprouts two Wili wings and a star on her forehead. After a few faltering steps she spins in delight at being able to dance again.

Footsteps are heard and the Wilis disappear. Albrecht appears, no longer disguised as Loys, with Wilfrid, his squire. He lingers by Giselle's grave in an attitude of deep despair. Wilfrid entreats him to leave the dismal spot but Albrecht prefers his sweet sorrow and orders Wilfrid away. Giselle is so touched by Albrecht's misery—he is lying on her grave—that she approaches him. Albrecht sees her and tries to embrace her but she retreats. Albrecht chases her but Giselle, although obviously anxious to show that she still loves him, evades his grasp.

This passionate dance has not gone unnoticed by the rest of the Wilis who have evil designs on all men who chance their way. Fortunately for Albrecht, however, they suddenly catch sight of Hilarion. The Queen of the Wilis touches him with her sceptre and he is forced to dance, first with her and then, one by one, with the rest of the Wilis. He tries to escape but the Wilis encircle him and he staggers about, giddy and despairing. Gradually the Wilis lead him to the lake's edge and he tumbles in, to drown in the icy water.

The Wilis now turn to Albrecht but just as Queen Myrtha is about to touch him with her sceptre Giselle intervenes and propels him towards the cross over her grave. She tells him that he will be safe while he clings to the cross. Myrtha is momentarily defeated but she soon sees that Albrecht will not be able to resist the sight of Giselle dancing and she forces her to perform. After some indecision, Albrecht duly leaves the cross and he and Giselle dance together. In a frenzied *pas de deux* both dancers fly from one corner of the glade to the other and Albrecht is soon exhausted by his breath-taking leaps. Myrtha forces Giselle to dance on and Albrecht has to drag his weary limbs after her. The Wilis surround the pair and Albrecht is about to follow Hilarion

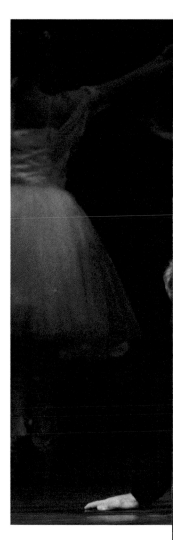

Marguerite Porter as Giselle and David Wall as Albrecht at the end of the grand pas de deux, Act II. Kirov Ballet, 1979

into the lake when four o'clock strikes and the dawn begins
to break. The Wilis start to droop and fade. Giselle gently
frees herself from Albrecht's arms and, as if in a dream,
moves slowly towards her grave. Albrecht pulls himself
together and sweeps her up to lay her on a bank of flowers.
He kneels and kisses her hand as Giselle slowly disappears
into the earth.

Albrecht is distraught as Wilfrid enters the glade with
Bathilde and her father. Giselle's last gesture is towards
Bathilde whom she wishes Albrecht to love in her place.
Albrecht faints in the arms of Bathilde as the curtain falls.

Romantic Ballet

On 23 July 1827 Marie Taglioni danced for the first time at the Paris Opéra. It was a momentous occasion and more than anything marks the beginning of the great age of Romantic ballet. The period of the flashy, virtuoso, male-dominated style of dance popular since the late eighteenth century was over and now began what *Le Constitutionel* of 27 July 1840 called 'a revolution against the rule of the pirouette, but a revolution that was greatly accomplished, through the irresistible power of grace, perfection and beauty in the art. Marie Taglioni loosened the legs, softened the muscles, gradually changed by her example the taste-less routine and unstylish attitudes, taught the art of seductive poses and correct and harmonious lines, and founded the double kingdom of grace and strength, the most beautiful and most pleasing and rarest of kingdoms.' This new style of dancing, ethereal, airy, remote, was perfectly able to express the Romantic pursuit of the unattainable. The great Romantic ballets such as *La Syl-phide* (1832) and *Giselle* (1841) rely for their dramatic impact on the helpless love of a mortal for a fairy or similar spirit. However the dramatic impact would have been negligible had the fairy not been seen to move in an ethereal way. The Romantic ballet technique perfected by Taglioni made the Romantic dream a theatrical reality. Taglioni's great contribution to ballet technique was the integration of point work within the framework of the ballet as a whole. For some years ballerinas such as Avdotia Istomina and Amalia Brugnoli had astounded audiences with *tours de force* on the very tip of their toes, but Taglioni was the first to give the new technique expressive power. As a result the Romantic ballet had its own expressive language.

Of course the mere fact that Taglioni got up on her toes did not constitute the overnight creation of Romantic ballet. It was a gradual process which merely started with Tag-lioni's début at the Opéra. In fact ballet was one of the slowest of the arts to respond to the spirit of Romanticism that swept Europe at the end of the eighteenth century. Painting, music and literature were quick to adapt to the more general feeling of revolution and change and all began to question the academic strictures of the previous two centuries. Greater emphasis on the individuality of expression freed technique from a formality in all the arts and stimulated a fascination with experimentation.

In France, where the observance of academic rules in the arts had been a matter of government policy and national pride since the days of Louis XIV, the Romantic reaction

Amalia Brugnoli and her husband, Paolo Samengo, in L'Anneau Magique. Lithograph after Levasseur, 1832. The ballet was first performed in 1832 in London with choreography by Ferdinand Albert. Mme Brugnoli had been dancing on her points since 1822 and by the 1830s there was fierce rivalry between her and Fanny Elssler

had been particularly violent. For instance the traditional unities of the French tragic theatre and general politeness of French literary style were transformed through the influence of Byron, Scott, Goethe, Schiller and Shakespeare. The Anglo-Saxon influence was particularly important in developing a new interest in non-classical history, exotic settings and mysterious events, especially in that most popular form of Romantic theatre, the melodrama, with its bold emphasis on local colour, ghosts and other supernatural beings. It was but a step from the crudities of spoken melodrama, with its musical accompaniment, to silently mimed ballet where mystery and magic could be shown much more convincingly and with more sophistication.

The convincing illusion of the Romantic ballet was made possible by the simultaneous development of its four components: drama, music, scenery and choreography. The first ballet at the Opéra to have a dramatic plot specifically created for the purpose was *La Somnambule* (1827) with a scenario by Eugène Scribe. Before this the usual practice had been for the choreographer to transcribe more or less literally the action of an existing book or play such as *Le Page inconstant* or *Cendrillon*, both seen at the Opéra in 1823. Before this the *ballets d'action* of the late eighteenth century had been based largely on classical myth. Even *La Sylphide* was based very loosely on a novel, Charles Nodier's *Trilby*. Scribe and Vernoy de Saint-Georges became the most prolific of the ballet librettists, adding to their fecundity in other literary fields, and writers like Théophile Gautier added the necessary touch of poetic vision. Romantic ideas of long ago and far away were

Left
The foyer of the Paris Opéra, in about 1850. Anonymous drawing in watercolour and gouache

fulfilled with subjects like *La Gypsy* of 1839, set in Edinburgh during the reign of Charles II, and *La Péri* of 1843, set in an exotic Egypt of indeterminate date. The other Romantic passion for ghosts by moonlight found its first expression at the Opéra in the ballet of the spectral nuns in Meyerbeer's opera *Robert le Diable* of 1831 and the triumph of poetic mystery was most perfectly expressed in *La Sylphide* of the following year.

    La Sylphide was one of the first ballets to have any strong sense of musical atmosphere. The composer, Jean-Madeleine Schneitzhoeffer, inherited a rather slapdash tradition of ballet music in which original ideas were thrown together with renditions of well-known tunes to form a danceable pot-pourri of unrelated musical ideas. A greater composer, and, for a time, Schneitzhoeffer's

Above
A scene from Act II of La Gypsy with Adèle Dumilatre and Jean Coralli. According to Théophile Gautier, Fanny Elssler surpassed herself in the famous Cracovienne dance in the ballet and achieved great popularity in the role

superior at the Opéra, Ferdinand Hérold, produced a number of ballet scores including *La Somnambule* and in 1828 a new version of the forty-year-old ballet, *La Fille mal gardée*. Hérold was a frustrated composer of grand opera but as a writer of both comic operas and ballets he was very much the mentor of Adolphe Adam who acknowledged his debt: 'All those who write music for the dance will seek to do it as well as he. No one will be able to do it better.' François Halévy and Ambroise Thomas are best known as opera composers but their contribution to Romantic ballet music, especially to Adolphe Adam's work, was considerable. Thomas's *La Gypsy* of 1839 marked a return to a form of *ballet d'action* in which the mime sections contribute as much as the more lyrical passages. This dualism is one of the great strengths of Adam's *Giselle*. Halévy's

The 'floating Wili' in Giselle *Act II. The truth revealed in* Magic: Stage Illusions and Scientific Diversions *by A. A. Hopkins, 1897*

Manon Lescaut of 1830 included perhaps the earliest use of leitmotiv in a ballet score and the manipulation and re-colouring of Manon's theme is the major precursor of Adam's skillful use of the device in *Giselle*.

The Paris Opéra had always been the home of spectacular theatrical effect and the new building in the rue Le Peletier, which opened on 16 August 1821 and was destroyed in 1873, had the finest scenic resources. Unfortunately scenic resource was not matched by scenic invention and in the 1820s productions at the Opéra were still graced by rich, symmetrical baroque sets reminiscent of the early eighteenth century. Cleverly lit and atmospheric Romantic sets had been seen in London since the 1780s, and by 1820 the Paris boulevard theatres battled for success with illusionistic effects and Romantic fantasy. The introduction of gas lighting made gradual lighting variations possible and created a living picture out of the stage behind the proscenium arch – it was now possible to lower the house lights and keep the audience in expectant darkness.

In April 1827 the Opéra convened a committee to bring the scenic department up to date. The principal administrative figure for much of the first half of the nineteenth century was Henri Duponchel but the genius of scenic design at the Opéra was Pierre Ciceri. He had joined the Opéra as a painter of landscape scenery as early as 1809 and had provided sets for a number of very good productions including *Alfred le Grand*, seen in Paris in 1822, but it was through Duponchel's influence that Ciceri developed into the most important stage designer of the Romantic period in France. His sets for Rossini's *Guillaume Tell* of 1829 were of an atmospheric complexity hitherto unknown at the Opéra and the cloister scene for Meyerbeer's *Robert le Diable* marks a climax of Romantic scenery design in France. Théophile Gautier thought the mysterious set as important as Meyerbeer's music in creating the shattering effect produced by the opera and Ciceri's later sets, especially for the second acts of *La Sylphide* and *Giselle*, were seen as the perfect expression of the Romantic vision of obscure mystery, rich and strange.

Ballet technique advanced, one might say, in leaps and bounds in the early decades of the nineteenth century. The athleticism of the male dancers was the principal attraction, with particular attention being paid to the increasing number of turns possible in a pirouette. It was the development of the more poetic possibilities of the female dancer, however, that was ultimately of more significance to the history of ballet in general and the development of the

Romantic ballet in particular. Point work, like the endless pirouette, began as a sort of circus turn with a pose held on tiptoe to give an illusion of lightness. As dancing on full point became an integral part of new choreography the expressive power of the technique became apparent.

Taglioni's ethereal, fairy-like qualities matched the increasing illusion of light and scenery, the atmospheric qualities of the music and the exotic mystery of many Romantic libretti. Her importance was recognized immediately and Le Figaro of 13 August 1827 was one of the first to acknowledge it: 'Her début will open a new epoch. It is Romanticism applied to the dance . . .'.

However, despite her celebrity, Taglioni was only one of several leading dancers at the Opéra and it was not until 1 August 1831 that her supremacy was rewarded with a salary of 30,000 francs. The decision to elevate Taglioni as a sort of figure-head of the Romantic ballet was taken by Louis Véron, the new director of the Opéra. He had taken over the running of the theatre after the 1830 revolution against the restored Bourbon monarchy when the cost of running the theatre was removed from the privy purse and became the concern of a subsidized private enterprise. Véron had strong ideas on the ballet which perfectly express the more down-to-earth side of the Romantic ballet: ' . . .in a ballet the public demands above all a varied and striking score, new and unusual costumes, a great variety, contrasting sets, surprises, transformation scenes, and a simple plot which is easy to follow and in which the dance develops naturally out of the situations. To all that must be added the charm of a young, beautiful dancer who dances differently and better than those who have preceded her.'

The history of the Romantic ballet does tend to be written in terms of the 'young and beautiful dancer who dances differently and better than those who have preceded her', especially in the decade that separates Marie Taglioni's performance in La Sylphide and Carlotta Grisi's in Giselle. The greatest dancer of all was undoubtedly Fanny Elssler, whose fiery qualities and brilliant mime technique made her the perfect antidote to Taglioni's filmy intangibility. Her performances as the dumb girl, Fenella, in Auber's opera La Muette de Portici and as Florinda, the cachucha dancer in the ballet Le Diable boîteux, choreographed by Coralli, had a full-blooded quality that Théophile Gautier saw as 'an air of Spanish vivacity tempered by a German simplicity'. It was the opposing qualities of Taglioni and Elssler that Grisi attempted to combine in Giselle, the consummation of the early Romantic ballet.

Marie Taglioni in La Sylphide. *Lithograph after A. E. Chalon. First performed at the Paris Opéra in March 1832, the ballet appeared in July at the Theatre Royal in London. Taglioni's white muslin dress was the first of a series of costumes designed for Romantic ballets and was the precursor of the* tutu *which became the conventional costume of the ballerina*

The Origins of Giselle

Giselle, ou Les Wilis, a ballet-pantomime in two acts, was first performed at the Paris Opéra on Monday 28 June 1841. It followed a performance of the third act of Rossini's *Moïse* and was the brainchild of Théophile Gautier, the romantic poet and aesthete whose theories on art and literature had such a strong influence on European culture of the nineteenth century. He was, in turn, inspired by another Romantic poet, the German Heinrich Heine. Gautier's notice of the first performance of *Giselle* takes the form of an open letter to Heine in which he recalls his moment of inspiration for the ballet—his first reading of the German poet's *De l'Allemagne*: 'I came across an exquisite passage—only a matter of opening the book at any page—where you speak of sprites in white gowns with hems that are perpetually damp, fairies whose little satin feet mark the ceiling of the wedding bedroom, the snow-white Wilis who waltz the whole night long, and wondrous apparitions encountered in the Harz mountains and on the banks of the Ilse, glimpsed in a mist bathed by German moonlight. "What a charming ballet all this would make", I thought quite spontaneously.'

Heinrich Heine adapted his idea of the Wilis from Slavonic legend. According to his version the Wilis are maidens engaged to be married but who die before their wedding day. They are unable to rest peacefully in their graves because while they were alive they could not satisfy their passion for dancing. Therefore, they foregather at midnight and lure any available young man to dance with them until he drops dead.

Heine's version of the Wilis was a Romantic one. They are much more complex creatures than he suggested and their nature varies depending upon the source of the legend. All agree that they are the souls of the departed but their precise nature varies. In Serbia they were maidens cursed by God, but in Bulgaria, where they were known as *samovily*, they were girls who had died unbaptized. Heine's version owes most to the Slav legend in which they are the souls of brides who died after their betrothal. He also recalls the Polish *wily*, the souls of beautiful young girls who float in the air between earth and sky to atone for their frivolous lives.

Gautier visualized a ballet in two acts with the Wilis playing the principal part in the second. His problem was how to transform the heroine of the first act into a dead Wili in the second. First of all, he turned to Victor Hugo's poem 'Fantômes', in his collection *Les Orientales*, in which a young girl dies of a chill after dancing all night in a hot

Right
'Les Wilis'. Lithograph by M. Fassoli after A. Cendron

Above
Theophile Gautier (1811– 72), photographed by Nadar in about 1857

ballroom. Gautier developed this idea and introduced the Queen of the Wilis early in the first act. She touches the floor of the ballroom with her wand to ensure that the dancers exhaust themselves completely, and then touches Giselle's heart with her cold hand as she leaves the ball at dawn.

E42813

This idea would not have transferred well to the stage as it would have come across as nothing more than a series of dances with a somewhat irrelevant dramatic touch at the end. Gautier, much more of a poet than a playwright, needed professional assistance and he turned to Jules-Henri Vernoy, Marquis de Saint-Georges. Vernoy de Saint-Georges was a professional dandy and a prolific writer for all occasions; before he assisted Gautier with *Giselle* he had written the libretti for nine comic operas, one grand opera and two ballets, *La Gypsy* of 1839 and *Le Diable amoureux* of 1840. He went on to script twelve ballets and no less than eighty operas. His fertile imagination quickly produced the setting and the story-line for the first act of *Giselle* and he probably carried his strong sense of theatrical organization into the second act. Thus, in three days it seems, the two men produced the libretto for what has always been recognized as the perfect Romantic ballet; dramatic and poetic, alternating simple rusticity and mysterious other-worldliness. The director of the Opéra, Leon Pillet, accepted the synopsis straightaway but rather than trying to secure a composer and a choreographer he seems to have left the initial organization to Saint-Georges.

Carlotta Grisi and Jules Perrot in La Polka. *Performed in Prague in 1835, the polka became popular in Paris during 1840. Perrot and Grisi demonstrated the dance as a divertissement in London in 1844*

Gautier was desperately keen to have Carlotta Grisi dance the heroine in his ballet. He had admired her talent, with its combination of Marie Taglioni's lyricism and Fanny Elssler's fire, since seeing her Opéra début on 12 February 1841 in a *divertissement* in Donizetti's opera *La Favorite*. 'She has strength, lightness, suppleness and an originality of style which immediately place her between Elssler and Taglioni.' He approached her teacher and common-law husband, Jules Perrot, with the libretto of *Giselle* and was thrilled when Perrot recognized that the ballet would be the ideal vehicle for Grisi's talents.

Perrot took the libretto of *Giselle* to his friend the composer Adolphe Adam who had just finished another ballet score, *La Jolie Fille de Gand*, originally intended for Pauline Leroux. Her illness, however, led to the ballet being offered to Grisi. The ballet was already in rehearsal but Grisi was not entirely happy with her role which was too long and did not allow her to show off her dancing as well as she might wish; the ballet was to be her début in a full-length work at the Opéra, a much more significant occasion than her actual first apearance which was merely a *pas de deux* (with Lucien Petipa) in the middle of the opera. At Adam's behest the production of *La Jolie Fille de Gand* was delayed and he wrote the full score for *Giselle* in the extraordinarily short space of three weeks.

The Music

Adolphe Adam was born in Paris in 1803, the son of a professor of music at the Conservatoire. He entered the Conservatoire himself when he was seventeen and by the time he was twenty was writing songs for the Parisian vaudeville theatres. He helped Boïeldieu with his opera *La Dame blanche* in 1825 and toured Belgium, Holland, Germany and Switzerland the following year. In Geneva he met Eugène Scribe, the most prolific French playwright and librettist of the nineteenth century, with whom he collaborated on a number of operas over the next thirty years. Adam died, quite exhausted, in 1856. In all he wrote seventy operas including a *Henry V* in 1830, and a *Falstaff* in 1856; the most popular were *Le Chalet* of 1834 and *Le Postillon de Longjumeau* of 1836. Apart from his obvious industry Adam was also possessed of an unusual musical facility that was perhaps better suited to the rhythms of ballet music than to more demanding operatic or religious

Above
Adolphe Adam. Lithograph after H. Adam

Left
Louise Fleury in La Jolie Fille de Gand. *Lithograph after A. E. Chalon. The dancer is probably dressed in the role of Beatrix in Act III, Scene 1 of the ballet*

compositions. He produced fourteen ballets, beginning with *La Chatte blanche* in 1830 and finishing with *Le Corsaire*, writted in 1856, the year of his death. *Giselle* was by far the most successful although *La Fille du Danube* of 1836, *La Jolie Fille de Gand*, performed in 1842, *Le Diable à quatre* of 1845 and *Le Corsaire* were also very popular.

Like everything else that Adam wrote, the music for *Giselle* was composed quickly and at night. Adam, in his memoirs, cannot remember how long he took to compose *Giselle* but three weeks seems most probable. The music is pleasant and danceable. Its local colour relates very closely to the varying moods of the libretto. The forceful yet sympathetic use of leitmotiv for the various characters and emotions prevents Adam's score from ever sinking into the inconsequential blandness of much nineteenth-century French ballet music.

The brief orchestral introduction, with its delineation of a pitiless fate, contrasts dramatically with the lyrical melody we hear once the curtain has risen; but we have been warned that this is not to be an untroubled love story. Despite the bold opening, however, Adam's orchestration is only on occasion overtly dramatic and he frequently relies on lyrical dialogue between wind instruments backed

Above
Music cover for a set of quadrilles from Adam's music for La Jolie Fille de Gand *adapted by Musard*

up by string accompaniment. The flute invariably makes its presence felt during the more dramatic moments.

Albrecht's theme in C major is matched by one for Giselle in G major, which becomes the first love theme, heard as the lovers pluck the petals of the daisy. Hilarion is given a suitably sinister E minor theme which is dispelled by the villagers, who interrupt the reproaches of Hilarion with a jolly rustic allegro, made all the more jolly by the tingling of a triangle. Another rustic dance modulates into an A major allegro that becomes the main love theme of Albrecht and Giselle.

Adam's stream of pretty tunes is never inconsequential but he forces the music to take itself a little more seriously with the entrance of Berthe and the ensuing, fairly lengthy, passage of mime. He paints in very precise orchestral colours the tension between mother and daughter. When Berthe mentions the terrible Wilis, their chromatic theme is heard mysteriously on flute, oboe and bassoon; the violins accompany with a tremulando. The whole passage of Berthe's mime is of the greatest importance as it brings together, in clear musical detail, the two sides of the ballet, the bright gaiety of the peasants' life in the first act and the sinister gloom of the Wilis in the second.

Above
A page from Adam's original score for Giselle *showing the music for the grand waltz, Act I*

Right
Galina Mezentseva as Giselle *and Konstantin Zaklinsky as Albrecht in the mad scene of* Giselle *Act I. Kirov Ballet, 1979*

The hunting party arrive to suitable trumpet and horn calls reminiscent of Weber, and another mime scene, this time between Giselle and the elegantly dressed Bathilde, is closely depicted in the music.

In most peformances this is the moment chosen to insert a peasant *pas de deux* by Frédéric Burgmüller. It takes the form of a set of five dances interpolated into the original production to please a wealthy patron of the Opéra whose mistress, Nathalie Fitzjames, took the part of the peasant girl. Nor is the next part of the ballet by Adam. Giselle's variation, in which she dances before the assembled crowd on stage, was composed by Minkus. It was introduced by Adam into the original score and quickly became such a familiar piece of bravura choreography that it has been retained in subsequent productions.

With Hilarion's angry interruption Adam once again takes over and follows with his usual precision the mime of accusation, denial and final proof. Giselle's retreat into madness, the greatest mime scene in Romantic ballet, is closely followed by the musical recapitulation of her love for Albrecht. The first love theme reappears, slower and more hesitant than before, and is then brutally cut short by a dramatic transition into a violent allegro. Then the

Above
Music cover for Frédéric Burgmüller's waltz from Le Souvenir de Ratisbonne, *part of the peasant* pas de deux *introduced into Act I*

second, more familiar, love theme appears, still in A major but disjointed in rhythm and interrupted by mad screams on the flute. Adam does not merely repeat the earlier themes in their related minor keys, he chooses the much more difficult method of changing the rhythm and tempo of the themes and altering the orchestral colour. Nevertheless, there is a final modulation into E and D minor and Giselle dies to a concluding fortissimo. Adam's music is an exact counterpart of the dramatic libretto and choreography and their perfect integration is what marks *Giselle* as the masterpiece of the Romantic ballet.

The mood of the second act is, of course, quite different from that of the first and the music is much more fluid and integrated than the somewhat episodic thematic music of the first act. The first bars of the music set the mood for the remainder of the ballet; oboes, clarinets and bassoons reply to the French horns, trumpets and trombones against a tremulando background of strings. This mysterious mood is interrupted by Hilarion's theme as he contemplates Giselle's grave and the love theme is recalled plaintively.

Midnight strikes, the twelve strokes emphasized by flutes, clarinets and strings; we hear the menacing music of the Wilis and then the flight of the huntsmen. A series of arpeggios on the harp marks the entrance of Myrtha, Queen of the Wilis. Her music, and that for her followers, is all written in the same undulating, singing phrases passing to and fro between flute and strings. Myrtha's initial solo is set to a lilting 3/4 time theme in B flat major, with the clarinets strengthening the flute and harp accompaniment. She then moves into an andantino in A flat with the violin theme echoed by the flute. Several arpeggios on the harp announce a waltz in A flat and E flat during which Myrtha summons her Wilis.

The Wilis are announced by a subliminal phrase on the cor anglais, accentuated by oboes and flutes. The Wilis 3/4 andantino, followed by a 6/8 moderato in E flat, acts as a subdued and gracious introduction to the entry of Giselle. She appears slowly from her grave and when touched by Myrtha's wand flings herself into a D major moderato, the oboes rushing repeatedly up one and a half octaves.

Albrecht enters to a minor theme on the oboe which reflects his utter misery. A quick allegro intervenes as Wilfrid tries to persuade Albrecht to leave the glade but the theme on the oboes returns when Wilfrid leaves, this time accompanied by the Wilis' music. Giselle appears and the two lovers begin to dance to music similar to that for the *pas de deux* in the first act. However, by using different rhythms

Galina Mezentseva as Giselle and Konstantin Zaklinsky as Albrecht in the grand pas de deux, Giselle Act II. Kirov Ballet, 1979

and tonal colour, Adam creates a totally different mood.

A shrieking note of aggression in the violins announces the return of Hilarion, chased by the Wilis. He is finally hounded into the lake after attempting to dance to a demonic rondo. The music calms down as Myrtha addresses her next victim, Albrecht. In orchestral terms he is now represented by the oboe, and Giselle, in her new role of protectress, by the viola. The grand *pas de deux* in E flat is the closest the music of the second act gets to the joyful exuberance of the first. The variation for Giselle by Minkus was first inserted in the 1864 Paris production and has kept its place in subsequent revivals. It uses the first love theme of the first act and is followed by a recapitulation of the E flat theme in which the Wilis force Albrecht to dance.

The imminent death of Albrecht is marked by a descending phrase in E minor but the dawn clock strikes and the violins respond with a majestic theme in D flat major. Giselle's final descent into her grave is accompanied by the softest orchestration but the ballet ends with a loud and passionate allegro.

The Choreography

Adam's music for *Giselle* follows the libretto of the ballet so precisely and with such apt local colour that one feels he must have collaborated closely with the choreographer. It comes as rather a surprise to learn that the identity of the choreographer of *Giselle* was a matter of uncertainty even at the time of the first performance. Jules Perrot, who took the libretto to Adam in the first place, is the most obvious candidate but his status outside the Opéra hierarchy made official recognition difficult.

In 1841 the ballet of the Paris Opéra was the finest and most celebrated in Europe. There were ten male and thirteen female soloists, including many of the finest dancers of the day, backed up by a *corps de ballet* of sixty-four. Most of the new choreography, both for the ballets proper and for the *divertissements* in opera, was prepared by the two ballet masters, Jean Coralli and Joseph Mazilier. Coralli was the senior of the two and he was officially responsible for the choreography of *Giselle*. Although born in Paris in 1779, he was of Italian origin and his outlook was cosmopolitan. He made his début as a dancer at the Opéra in 1802 but spent the next twenty years choreographing all over Europe. He was made ballet master to the

Above
Jean Coralli (1779–1854).
Lithograph after C. Vogt,
1858
Below
A handbill announcing the
first performance of Giselle

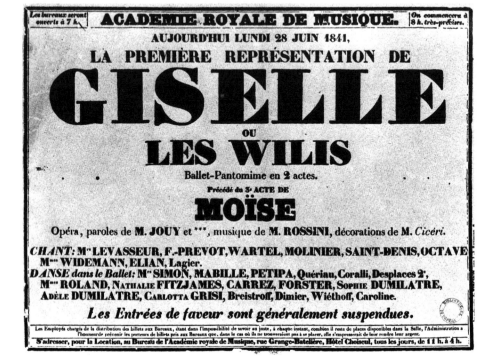

Théâtre de la Porte Saint-Martin in Paris in 1826 and ballet master to the Opéra in 1831. At the Opéra his ballets included *La Tempête* of 1834, *Le Diable boîteux* of 1836 and *La Chatte métamorphosée en Femme* of 1837.

According to the posters and publicity for the first performance of *Giselle* Coralli was the sole choreographer but contemporary sources make it quite clear that much of the credit must go to Jules Perrot. Adam, describing the première in a letter to Vernoy de Saint-Georges, says that much of the success was due to Perrot, and the reviewer in *La Revue dramatique* of 1 July 1841 is even more specific: 'One must add that although the playbill makes no mention of it, M. Perrot arranged all his wife's dances himself and is thus author of a large part of the ballet'. Officially, Grisi was Perrot's wife and the Opéra records show that her salary was paid to her as Mme Perrot.

Just how much of *Giselle* was choreographed by Coralli and how much by Perrot has caused a great deal of speculation. It seems reasonable, however, to accept contemporary comment in giving all Giselle's solos and scenes to Perrot, and Adam's word, again in the letter to Vernoy de Saint-Georges, that Coralli was responsible for the dances of Myrtha and the Wilis. The great mime scene of Giselle's madness was undoubtedly originally choreo-

Carlotta Grisi and Jules Perrot in Le Rossignol, *the ballet in which Perrot made his début at the Paris Opéra on 23 June 1830*

graphed by Perrot and the other, rather tedious, mime scenes were probably arranged by Coralli. The scene between Hilarion and the Wilis is probably by Perrot because of its similarity to the scene of the capture of Medora in Perrot's 1858 version of Mazilier's *Le Corsaire*.

But why should Perrot's contribution to the choreography of *Giselle* be so equivocal? Was his work opposed by the directorate of the Opéra or were they hoping to use his intimacy with Grisi to their non-paying advantage? Perrot

Carlotta Grisi as Esmeralda and Jules Perrot as Gringoire in La Esmeralda. *Lithograph after J. Bouvier. The background shows Paris in the fourteenth century*

was a familiar figure at the Opéra. His first appearance there, in May 1830, had surprised balletomanes who had previously regarded him as a brilliant acrobat. His acrobatic training did, in fact, give him an unequalled lightness and springiness of movement and he was probably the one male dancer able to match the ease and elevation of the great ballerinas of the Romantic era. However, he was sensible enough to see that the great pre-Romantic age of the male dancer was over and that the prima ballerina was the new focal point of ballet. After five years at the Opéra he toured the opera houses of Europe with considerable success and, in 1836, while appearing at the Teatro San Carlo in Naples, came across a seventeen-year-old dancer called Carlotta Grisi. Perrot immediately saw her potential, not only as a prima ballerina but also as a future partner for himself—a possible extension of his own career. It may be a mistake to read too much into Perrot's actions but he did succeed in making his find into one of the great ballerinas of the mid-nineteenth century.

The greatest moment of Grisi's career was her performance as Giselle, and Perrot might have been willing to sacrifice any recognition for himself on seeing that the ballet was the perfect vehicle for his protégée. On the other hand, he might have seen Grisi's potential triumph as the means of access to a position for himself on the staff of the Opéra. Anybody who mattered would know who had really choreographed the ballet; Grisi's performance would show him to be a choreographer of genius and a necessary addition to the staff of the Opéra, so why not let Coralli, the official choreographer, take the official praise?

Assigning the choreography of Giselle to both Coralli and Perrot, however, does not completely solve the problems surrounding the authorship of the ballet. The records of the Opéra show that only one man was paid to choreograph Giselle and he was Albert Decombe usually known simply as 'Albert'. He had partnered the famous ballerina, Mlle Bigottini, in the 1820s and he was working on the choreography of Adam's ballet La Jolie Fille de Gand in June 1841, the ballet that Grisi rejected in favour of Giselle. Albert had been appointed by Pillet in 1840 for two, four or six years, according to how well he pleased the administration, to oversee the production of all ballets and divertissements performed at the Opéra. The engagement was apparently kept a closely guarded secret and Albert never seems to have claimed any sort of credit for Giselle. He was, however, a well-known choreographer, and had been since his success with Sor's Cendrillon in 1823. It is curious that contemporaries did not mention his part in the creation of *Giselle* and the fascinating possibility remains that he was at least a collaborator with Coralli and Perrot.

The choreography of *Giselle* may be the work of several different hands—modern productions rely heavily on revisions made by Marius Petipa—but the result is a uniquely satisfying combination of dance and mime. The short mimed scenes of the first act culminate in Giselle's extraordinary mad scene and in the second act the mime is completely integrated into the dance. Apart from the mimetic gestures, which can be read like a book and followed closely in Adam's music there is also in *Giselle* an effective use of expressive gesture.

The dance steps, combinations and sequences in *Giselle* are relatively restricted but, this time following the lead of the music, there is a brilliant use of choreographic leitmotiv. Giselle shows her love of dancing with a series of *ballonnés piqués* followed by a *pas de basque*, a combination that reappears whenever her passion expresses itself; for example, when dancing for the villagers at the beginning

Below

Carlotta Grisi as Giselle, by J. Brandard. Her tomb, a lake and hills are in the background

of the first act and when she has her talk with Bathilde. Like the musical themes, this choreographic leitmotiv appears in a disjointed and disturbed version during the mad scene. In the second act the most important leitmotiv is the use of the *arabesque* by the Wilis. Myrtha introduces the theme in her solo and the Wilis use the *arabesque* in a number of ways in all their dances, the best known being the series of *temps levés en arabesque* when the Wilis are divided into two groups and dance towards and through each other. Giselle's moment of wakened ecstacy, when touched by Myrtha's wand, is expressed by her brilliant and rapid series of *temps levés en arabesque en tournant.*

Giselle remains one of the greatest pieces of sustained choreographic invention. Perrot, Coralli, perhaps Albert and certainly, at a later date, Petipa all contributed their respective genius or talent. The fact that several hands have been at work does not make *Giselle* particularly unusual amongst full-length ballets of any age but that the synthesis in *Giselle* is so successful is a tribute to the tightness of the libretto and the theatrical precision of Adam's music.

Below
The Wilis executing their series of temps levés en arabesque, Giselle *Act II.* *Kirov Ballet, 1979*

The Original Designs

The scenery for the first production of *Giselle* was designed by the great Pierre Ciceri, who was chief designer to the Opéra from 1815 to 1847 and was responsible for over 300 productions. *Giselle* was given two months of rehearsals, an extremely generous period for the mid-nineteenth century and far more than suggested by Gautier with his breathless impression that the ballet was produced almost overnight. However Ciceri did not find two months long enough to produce original sets for both acts and he concentrated on the setting for the second.

The set for the rustic first act was put together with elements from Adam's ballet *La Fille du Danube* of 1838. An engraving of the first act in *Les Beautés de l'Opéra* of 1845 shows the picturesque cottages of Giselle and Loys on either side of the stage with the distant vista of vineyards and feudal castle framed by two large trees. However quickly the set was thrown together it has remained the model for all subsequent productions of the ballet.

The set for the second act was of much more interest to Ciceri and he worked on it with enthusiasm. Documents in

Giselle and Albrecht dancing together, Giselle Act I. Engraving after J. B. Giraldon for Les Beautés de l'Opéra, 1845

NOTICE SUR GISELLE.

ISELLE est le premier ballet que Carlotta Grisi ait dansé à l'Opéra, où elle avait débuté par ce pas si brillant de *la Favorite*, qui est encore un des plus beaux fleurons de sa couronne chorégraphique. On se souvenait bien d'avoir vu, il y a quelques années, à la Renaissance, une charmante enfant qui jouait un rôle dans une pièce intitulée *Zingaro*; mais l'on ne savait pas si c'était une danseuse ou une chanteuse, car elle était l'une et l'autre. Une voix fraîche, pure et juste, une danse légère et correcte, de beaux yeux bleus d'une douce naïveté, voilà ce que Carlotta Grisi avait laissé dans la mémoire des gens du monde et des feuilletonistes. *Giselle* la plaça tout d'un coup au premier rang.

*Giselle, now a flying Wili,
evades the grasp of
Albrecht, Giselle Act II.
Engraving by J. Collignon
after J. B. Giraldon for* Les
Beautés de l'Opéra, *1845*

the archive of the Opéra show that each rush and branch was meticulously counted, decorated and measured to fit in with the general décor and to help disguise the machinery. There were over 200 rushes and 120 flowering branches. The prototypes for this set were Ciceri's famous glade for the second act of *La Sylphide* and the earlier abbey interior for the ghostly nuns in Meyerbeer's *Robert le Diable*. It was the quintessential Romantic setting—picturesque details combining with a general feeling of mystery.

The set was at the same time lush and sensual and the engraving of the second act published in 1845 suggests that the dancing area may have been reduced by the over-enthusiastic effusions of the designer. Most of the Wilis, including of course Giselle herself, arrived and disappeared through trap-doors but some were probably flown in. The flying equipment at the Opéra, extensively used in *La Sylphide* was extremely sophisticated. Another attempt at illusion did not turn out so successfully. It had been planned to create the effect of the still surface of the lake by using a parallel arrangement of mirrors. However, the idea was dropped on grounds of expense and not until 1863 was the ballet given two long mirrored surfaces to reflect the drooping trees of the set.

Gautier described the setting of the second act in a piece of particularly purple prose, emphasizing the sensuality and curious attractions of the scene rather than its horror and incipient dangers. 'The stage presents a picture of a forest on the banks of a small lake; there are tall pale trees, their roots springing from the undergrowth and the rushes. The water lilies spread their broad dark leaves over the still

Costume design by Paul Lormier for a huntsman, Giselle Act I, in the original production of 1841

surface of the water, silvered and shimmering under a mysterious moon. The reeds, sheathed in brown velvet, rustle and whisper with the intermittent breath of the night air. Languid, the flowers slowly open to exude the heavy, heady perfumes of the east, like the great broad blooms of Java that turn mad all those that come near. What atmosphere of fiery passion and burning sensuality flows through this hidden grove.'

The costumes for *Giselle*, at least those for the principal characters and probably those for the Wilis, were designed by Paul Lormier who was costume designer at the Opéra from 1831. He became head of the costume department in 1855 and retained the position until 1887. Like J. R. Planché in England, he was a serious student of historic costume. However, the period of the costumes in *Giselle* was dictated by the fact that 78 out of a total of 160 costumes were reused from previous productions. These productions seem to have been Rossini's *Guillaume Tell* of 1829, Berlioz's *Benvenuto Cellini* of 1838 and Mazilier's ballet *Le Diable amoureux* of 1840, all vaguely Renaissance in character. These costumes probably clothed the *corps de ballet* in the first act and the fleeting huntsmen of the second. Lormier's designs for the specially produced cos-

Costume design by Paul Lormier for Albrecht, Giselle Act II, in the original production of 1841

tumes survive, annotated with marginal notes. There is also a notebook listing all the materials and accessories needed to make the costumes.

Lormier's idea of simple peasant dress in the first act included a light brown velvet bodice with a bright yellow skirt for Giselle and a doublet of purple cloth and grey silk hose for Albrecht. Hilarion was more practically dressed with his woodland accoutrements of hunting knife and hunting horn; in the original production there was evidently no need for Hilarion to rush across the stage at the end of the first act in order to blow the Prince's horn. In the first act there is one moment when the plot turns on a point of costume but Lormier's design for Bathilde's riding-habit, which excites such admiration from Giselle, was rather disappointing: it was a rather dull costume of green velvet with plain white sleeves.

In the second act Albrecht's true aristocratic provenance was reflected in his costume of pale yellow velvet and white silk. His black velvet cap with a peacock feather was evidently Lormier's distinguishing mark of aristocratic elegance. The costumes for the Wilis relied heavily on those

Above
Sketch for a costume design by Alexandre Benois for Hilarion, Giselle Act I, probably Paris Opéra, 1924

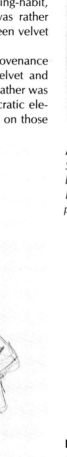

Left
Sketch for a costume design by Alexandre Benois for Giselle, Giselle Act I, probably Paris Opéra, 1924

designed by Eugène Lami for the fairies in *La Sylphide*, softening the lines of the body with layers of gauzy petticoats. Myrtha's white bodice with blue and silver wings and white skirt to below the knee was repeated in the costumes of all the other Wilis but only she had a garland of verbena and a star in the middle of her forehead.

Lormier's costumes were used at the Opéra until the ballet was withdrawn in 1853 although prints of Grisi as Giselle do tend to show her in a coquettish off-the-shoulder bodice rather than the one designed for her. For the revival of 1863 new costumes were designed by Alfred Albert. He followed the Renaissance feel of Lormier's costumes but added a certain heaviness of style that was attributed to the need for 'greater historical authenticity'. Albert's costumes were used until 1868 when the ballet was withdrawn from the repertoire of the Opéra and the next *Giselle* costumes designed for the Opéra were those by Alexandre Benois, produced for the 1924 performances. He, like Lormier and Albert, tried to be 'authentic' but succeeded only in watering down the Romanticism of the nineteenth-century costumes.

Above
Sketch for a costume design by Alexandre Benois for a huntsman, Giselle *Act I, probably Paris Opéra, 1924*

Left
Sketch for a costume design by Alexandre Benois for Albrecht, Giselle *Act I, probably Paris Opéra, 1924*

The Survival of Giselle

Giselle remained in the repertoire at the Opéra until 1849, with Grisi and Lucien Petipa always dancing the two principal roles. Petipa retained his part in the revivals of 1852 and 1853, playing opposite Mlle Guérinot and later Regina Forli. The ballet was then withdrawn until a revival in 1863 for the Paris début of Martha Muravieva, a Russian ballerina. There were frequent revivals—another Russian trained ballerina, Adela Grantzova, played Giselle in 1866 but after 1868 it was not seen at all in Paris until the Diaghilev Ballets Russes production in 1910 with Nijinsky and Karsavina. The next performances by the Opéra ballet company were not until 1924 when a production was mounted for the Russian ballerina, Olga Spessivtseva.

The Russian connection is evidently the fundamental cause for the survival of Giselle. Initially, however, the ballet was a huge international success. After the opening in Paris in 1841 productions were quickly mounted all over Europe. The first English performance was given at Her Majesty's Theatre on 12 March 1842 with Grisi as Giselle and Perrot as Albrecht. A performance at La Scala, Milan, followed on 17 January 1843 and although a French ballerina, Mlle Augusta, produced and performed Giselle in New York, at the Park Theatre, as early as 2 February 1842, the first American production was given in the Howard Athenaeum, Boston, on 1 January 1846. Much more significantly, the first Russian performance was given by the Imperial Ballet in St Petersburg on 18 December 1842.

Laure Fonta (above) and Martha Muravieva (below) in Giselle at the Paris Opéra in 1863

The Russian production was staged by Titus, the *maître de ballet*, who was sent to Paris in 1841 by Gedeonov, the director of the Imperial Theatre. His brief was to find a suitable vehicle for Yelena Andreyanova, the greatest Russian ballerina of the mid-nineteenth century, who was the Imperial Ballet's answer to Taglioni. In fact Andreyanova was particularly associated with the roles performed by Taglioni, and Gedeonov was anxious that she should slip out of the shadow of the ubiquitous Italian ballerina. Titus returned from Paris with Giselle but as he relied entirely on his own memory to reproduce the choreography, the production in St Petersburg varied considerably from the original. In 1843 Lucile Grahn gave two performances of Giselle in St Petersburg and was followed, in 1848, by Fanny Elssler.

The 1848 production was significant because Jules Perrot had just arrived in St Petersburg as *maître de ballet* to the Imperial Ballet, a position he retained until 1859, apart from a short period in 1851. He mounted a new production

Right
Lucien Petipa as Albrecht, Giselle Act I

of *Giselle* which Russian historians argue was the fulfilment of what had only been tentative beginnings in the original Paris performances. According to Natalia Roslavleva he strengthened the dramatic action of the ballet, deepened Giselle's mad scene and made all the secondary characters more convincing. Fanny Elssler was admired in the first act but was compared unfavourably with Andreyanova in the second act. Even when Carlotta Grisi danced her greatest role in St Petersburg in 1850 the memory of the Russian ballerina's interpretation was still preferred. The 1850 production was mounted by Marius Petipa for Grisi, under Perrot's supervision. It is probable that Petipa added his own touches to the choreography and continued to do so over the next forty years. In 1884 he may have changed quite fundamentally Coralli's choreography in the *grand pas de Wilis*. Petipa's changes to the choreography survive in modern productions of the ballet which, outside Russia, are based on the notations of Nikolay Sergeyev, *régisseur* at the Maryinsky Theatre.

When the Ballets Russes performed *Giselle* in Paris in 1910 it had not been seen outside Russia since the last Paris performances of 1868, when Albrecht was played by Mlle Sismondi. According to Benois the 1910 production was mounted with the idea of showing the great Pavlova to the French public in an ideal role. In the event it was Karsavina who played Giselle, partnered by Nijinsky as Albrecht. The ballet seems to have stunned the Paris audience as much as the more revolutionary Ballets Russes productions of 1910.

Benois designed the sets and costumes for the Diaghilev production. Initially he intended to give his designs a full-blooded Romantic feel, inspired by his childhood recollections of the ballet, but ultimately he lacked the courage of his convictions. 'I tried to create something that would answer the demands of a "sentimental reconstruction", but I very soon gave up the idea. I succeeded in making the two décors sufficiently "Romantic", but when it came to the costumes I became suddenly afraid that my idea of resuscitating old scenic images would be thought retrogressive and ridiculous, or a proof of the poverty of my imagination. I therefore decided, as a compromise, not to make use of the piquant possibilities of deliberate "lack of taste". Nijinsky's was the only costume I designed in exactly the correct style—the so-called troubadour style.'

In fact, Benois' 'correct' costume looked nothing like Lormier's original first-act costume for Albrecht but it was a design that was to have far-reaching consequences. Nijinsky's refusal to change from it into his usual costume in a subsequent St Petersburg production of *Giselle* led to his dismissal from the Imperial Ballet and his total commitment to Diaghilev's company.

Another Russian expatriate, Nikolay Sergeyev, assured the survival of the classical Russian repertoire in the West. When he left his position as *régisseur* to the Imperial Theatres in 1918 he took with him the notation of the entire repertoire of the Imperial Ballet. This move made Sergeyev the key figure in the development of the classical ballet repertoire in the West, and one of the earliest examples of Sergeyev's usefulness was the 1924 production of *Giselle* at

Vaslav Nijinsky as Albrecht and Tamara Karsavina as Giselle, Giselle *Act II Ballets Russes, Paris, 1910*

the Opéra. This was mounted for Olga Spessivtseva, perhaps the greatest Giselle of the twentieth century, and was an accurate reconstruction of the performance given by the Imperial Ballet.

The ballet was produced again in Paris in 1932 and in the same year the British Camargo Society decided to organize a production, given at the Savoy Theatre. Spessivtseva was induced to cross the channel and her Albrecht was Anton Dolin. The costumes and sets were those used by Pavlova's company. The production was evidently a success as eighteen months later, in 1934, Sergeyev was employed by Ninette de Valois to mount Giselle for her Vic-Wells Ballet with the company's first prima ballerina, Alicia Markova, in the title role and Anton Dolin again as Albrecht. Markova had seen both Spessivtseva and Pavlova dance Giselle but was not familiar with the role and had to be coached from scratch in the six weeks' rehearsal period. Margot Fonteyn took over the role in 1937 and continued to dance the part for the Vic-Wells, later the Royal Ballet, for nearly twenty-five years. Markova continued to play Giselle, first with her own company and then, from 1950, with London Festival Ballet. Dolin was her usual partner and he played Albrecht until 1959.

Above
Alicia Markova as Giselle
and Anton Dolin as
Albrecht, Giselle Act II.
Vic-Wells Ballet, 1934

Giselle is the great test-piece of the ballet repertoire. Every ballerina has to dance a convincing Giselle before she can be taken seriously, and the role has attracted the greatest dancers of the day. Natalia Makarova and Gelsey Kirkland of the American Ballet Theatre are among the

finest Giselles of recent years. Productions may vary in detail—for instance Mary Skeaping's six productions of the ballet changed as she did ever more research on origins and early productions—but as almost every step and gesture is as well known as the text of *Hamlet* it is perfectly easy to make comparisons. One of the most unusual was Arthur Mitchell's 'Creole' version for Dance Theatre of Harlem in 1984, set in the southern states of America. In 1984 at the Teatro Maliban in Venice Eva Evdokimova and Carla Fracci took part in a peculiar competitive entertainment in which they played, respectively, Fanny Elssler and Marie Taglioni. Although the part is not particularly associated with either of these two great Romantic ballerinas it was inevitable that the ultimate test was their interpretation of the role of Giselle. As they leaped across the stage with their partners from opposite corners in the *grand pas de deux* from act two of *Giselle* the competition suddenly made sense. All the earlier extracts from other ballets of the Romantic era became charming museum pieces; only *Giselle* retained the vitality, allure, mysticism and intensity of the Romantic movement.

Carla Fracci as Giselle in the film The Ballerina *produced by Joseph Wishy for Polivideo, 1985*

Index

Adam, Adolphe 16, 17, 22, 24, 25, 26, 27, 28, 30, 31, 33, 34, 35, 36
Albert, Alfred 41
Alfred le Grand 41
American Ballet Theatre 47
Andreyanova, Yelena 42
Augusta, Mlle 42
Les Ballets Russes 42, 44
Benois, Alexandre 41, 44, 45
Benvenuto Cellini 39
Berlioz, Hector 39
Bigottini, Mlle 34
Brugnoli, Amalia 12
Burgmüller, Frédéric 27
Cendrillon 14, 34
Le Châlet 24
La Chatte blanche 25
La Chatte metamorphosée en Femme 31
Ciceri, Pierre 17, 36, 37
Coralli, Jean 18, 30, 31, 32, 33, 34, 35, 44
Le Corsaire 25, 32
La Dame blanche 24
Dance Theatre of Harlem 47
Decombe, Albert 34
De Valois, Ninette 46
Le Diable amoureux 22, 39
Le Diable à quâtre 25
Le Diable boîteux 18, 31
Diaghilev, Serge 42, 44, 45
Dolin, Anton 46
Donizetti, Gaetano 22
Duponchel, Henri 17
Elssler, Fanny 18, 22, 42, 44
Evdokimova, Eva 47
Falstaff (Adam) 24
Fantômes 20
La Favorite 22
La Fille de Danube 25, 36
La Fille mal gardée 16
Fitzjames, Nathalie 27

Fonteyn, Margot 46
Forli, Regina 42
Fracci, Carla 47
Gautier, Théophile 14, 17, 18, 20, 21, 22, 36, 37
Grahn, Lucile 42
Grantzova, Adela 42
Grisi, Carlotta 18, 22, 31, 33, 34, 42, 44
Guillaume Tell 17, 39
La Gypsy 15, 16, 22
Halévy, François 16
Hamlet 47
Heine, Heinrich 20
Henry V (Adam) 24
Hérold, Ferdinand 16
Hugo, Victor 20
The Imperial Ballet 42, 45
Istomina, Avdotia 12
La Jolie Fille de Gand 22, 25, 34
Karsavina, Tamara 42, 44
Kirkland, Gelsey 47
Lami, Eugène 41
Leroux, Pauline 22
London Festival Ballet 46
Lormier, Paul 38, 40, 41, 45
Makarova, Natalia 47
Manon Lescaut (Halévy) 17
Markova, Alicia 46
Mazilier, Joseph 30, 32, 39
Meyerbeer, Giacomo 15, 17, 37
Mitchell, Arthur 47
La Muette de Portici 18
Muravieva, Martha 42
Nijinsky, Vaslav 42, 44, 45
Nodier, Charles 14
Les Orientales 20
Le Page inconstant 14
Paris. Opéra 12, 14, 15, 16, 17, 18, 20, 22, 30, 31, 33, 34, 36, 37, 38, 41, 42, 46
Paris. Théâtre de la Porte Saint-Martin 31

Pavlova, Anna 44, 46
La Péri 15
Perrot, Jules 22, 30, 31, 32, 33, 35, 42, 44
Petipa, Lucien 22, 42
Petipa, Marius 33, 35, 44
Pillet, Leon 22, 34
Le Postillon de Longjumeau 24
Robert le Diable 15, 17, 37
Roslavleva, Natalia 44
Rossini, Giacomo 17, 20, 39
The Royal Ballet 46
Saint-Georges, Vernoy de 14, 22, 31
Schneitzhoeffer, Jean-Madeleine 15, 16
Scribe, Eugène 14, 24
Sergeyev, Nikolay 44, 45, 46
Skeaping, Mary 47
La Somnambule 14, 16
Spessivtseva, Olga 42, 46
La Sylphide 12, 14, 15, 17, 18, 37
Taglioni, Marie 12, 18, 22, 42
La Tempête 31
Thomas, Ambroise 16
Trilby 14
Véron, Louis 18
The Vic-Wells Ballet 46
Weber, Carl Maria von 27

Acknowledgments
Bibliothèque de l'Opéra 6–7, 14, 21, 24, 26, 30, 38, 39, 43, 45; Jean-Loup Charmet 15; E. T. Archive 13, 19; John Gill 15, 25, 31, 34, 42; Marina Henderson Gallery, London 40, 41 Luciano Romano 47; Sothebys 46; Leslie Spatt 27, 29, 34–5; Theatre Museum 46; Victoria and Albert Museum 20, 22–3, 24, 34–5; Reg Wilson 10–11

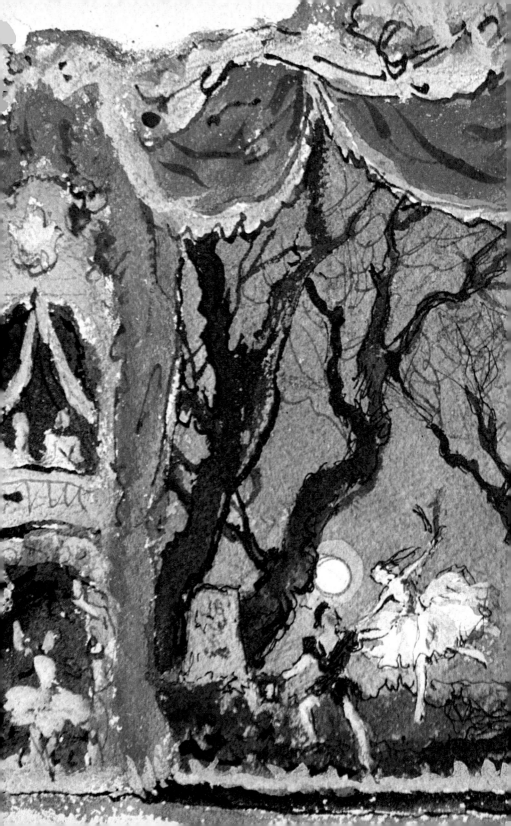